I am a
HINDU

I am a
HINDU

Manju Aggarwal
meets
Gaytri Devi Goswami

Photography: Chris Fairclough

Religious Consultant: A. T. S. Ratna Singham

FRANKLIN WATTS

LONDON/NEW YORK/SYDNEY/TORONTO

Gaytri Devi Goswami is eleven years old. She and her family are Hindu. Her father, Giriraj Prasad Goswami, is a Brahmin priest. Her mother, Shanti Devi, works in a factory in East London. Gaytri's sister Kunti is thirteen years old. Her brother Prem Raj is fourteen and Damoder, another brother, is sixteen. The family came to Britain in 1980 from India.

Contents

First published in the USA by
Franklin Watts Inc.
387 Park Avenue South
New York
N.Y. 10016
US ISBN: 0-531-10018-9
Library of Congress Catalog
  Card Number 85-50166
Printed in Hong Kong

The Publishers would like to
thank the Goswami family
and all other people shown
in this book. Special thanks
are also due to James
Pailing for his help and
encouragement in the
preparation of this book.

Manju Aggarwal is Co-
ordinator for South Asian
Languages for the London
Borough of Newham

A. T. S. Ratna Singham is
Chief Co-ordinator of the
Shri Ganapathy Temple in
Wimbledon, South London

The Hindu belief

My family follows a religion called Hinduism which began in India thousands of years ago.

Hinduism is one of the oldest religions in the world. Its beginnings can be traced back to 2500 BC in ancient India. The name Hindu was first used to describe the people who lived near the Indus River. The beliefs of these people became a religion and a way of life which spread throughout India.

**We believe that God can be seen
and worshipped in many ways.
Our family worships the god
Krishna.**

All Hindus believe there is one
supreme God called Brahman found
everywhere in the world. Some
believe that there are many gods who
are parts of the supreme God. These
gods look like humans or animals.
Each has different powers. Hindus
choose the ones they like best. Some
Hindus use other symbols, such as a
sacred flame, to worship God.

Worship at home

We have a prayer room in our home where we keep images of our gods. My father is a priest so we have many ceremonies to do.

Most Hindus have images or pictures of gods in their homes. Some homes, as here, have special rooms for worship. Gaytri's father is a Brahmin, a member of the Hindu priest class. He has chosen to spend all his time at home and worship his gods.

We begin the day by waking the gods and washing their images. My father puts tilak on his forehead.

The images of the gods are put in special small beds at night and on a platform during the day. There are different prayers to say and ceremonies to carry out with the gods throughout the day. Tilak is a religious symbol showing the particular belief of the wearer.

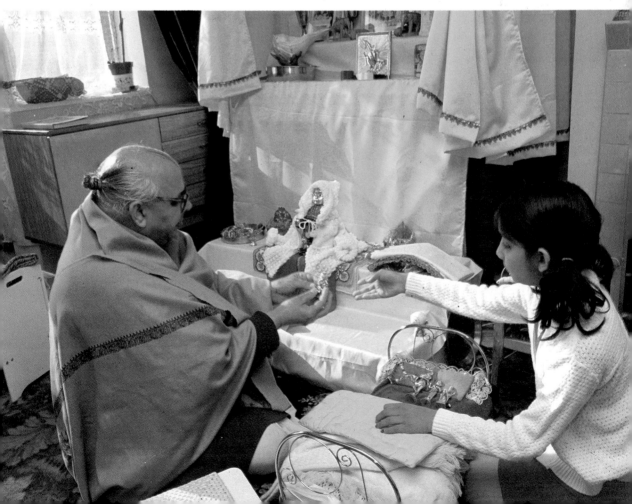

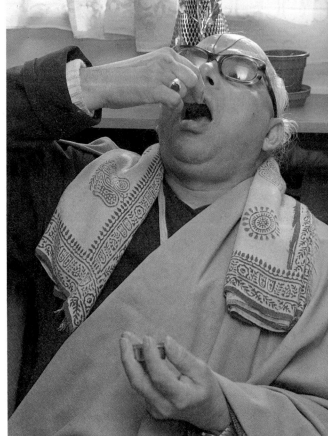

Daily worship and music

My father offers food to the gods in a special ceremony. He also prays and sings hymns.

The food offered to the gods becomes holy. When eaten by the worshipper it is called prasada. The person believes that the food has been shared with the gods. The same ceremony is done for all meals of the day. At night the gods are put back into their beds.

My father is a musician and a singer. I am learning to play the harmonium.

Most Hindus are very fond of music and it is used in many religious ceremonies. There are many different Indian musical instruments. Stringed instruments are more popular than wind instruments. The harmonium, shown in the picture, is like a small piano. Others are the sitar – a large stringed instrument like a guitar and the shennai, which is similar to the oboe.

Going to the Temple

We sometimes go to the temple to worship. Everybody has to take off their shoes to show respect.

As Hindus believe that God is everywhere, they can worship both at home or in a temple, called a mandir. For many the home is the main place of worship. Each temple has a main god, but there are always images of several other gods. Ganesha, the elephant-headed god, is the main god in the temple shown here. Prayers are said in front of a sacred flame.

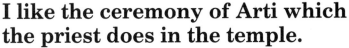

I like the ceremony of Arti which the priest does in the temple.

The priest holds a tray with five candles and moves it slowly in front of a god. Then the tray is brought around to everybody in the temple. The people hold their hands over the candles. Then they pass their hands over their forehead and hair. Offerings of money are made and the holy food prasada is eaten. During Arti hymns are sung to show love and devotion to God. The sacred word OM (above right) is chanted.

The Hindu gods

There are many beautiful statues of our gods in the temple. We respect them all although our family god is Krishna.

Each god is said to be a different part of the supreme God. A Hindu has to choose which one to worship. Vishnu is thought to be gentle and kind. He has many different human and animal forms. One of these is Krishna (below left), who appeared on earth to save mankind.

Shiva (left, in the circle) is thought to be a fierce god who rules life and death. Shiva also has many different forms. Some of these are goddesses such as Kali and Durga (above left) who have great power. Ganesha (above right), the elephant-headed god, is prayed to when starting something, like moving into a new house. Hindus also believe that things in nature are forms of God. The River Ganges in India is said to be holy. Pilgrims go to bathe in the river and wash away their sins.

The Holy Books

My father reads the Holy Books to us every day. I am also learning Sanskrit.

Hinduism has several Holy Books. The oldest are called the Vedas. These are collections of hymns which tell about the nature of the world and how to worship gods. For thousands of years they were not written down but learned by memory by all children of the Brahmin (priest) class. They were then written down in Sanskrit.

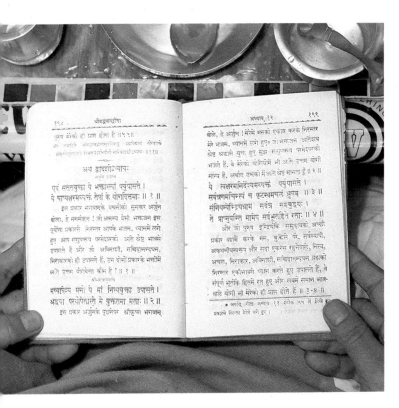

The Hindi Script

A अ	Ā आ	I इ	Ī ई	U उ
Ū ऊ	RI ऋ	Rī ॠ	LRI ॡ	
É ए	AI ऐ	O ओ	AU औ	(M) अं
H अः	K क	KH ख	G ग	GH घ
Ṅ ङ	C च	CH छ	J ज	JH झ
Ṅ ञ	Ṭ ट	ṬH ठ	Ḍ ड	ḌH ढ
Ṇ ण	T त	TH थ	D द	DH ध
N न	P प	PH फ	B ब	BH भ
M म	Y य	R र	L ल	V(W) व
SH श	Ṣ ष	S स	H ह	KSH क्ष
TR त्र	JÑ(GÑ) ज्ञ			

When I am older I will read the Upanishads. They are too difficult for me at present.

The Upanishads explain the place of man in the universe. They say that a person can be born again after death. One's actions in this life will affect what form, human or animal, one will be reborn into. After a perfect life one will be freed from birth and death to join God. Later writings such as the Bhagavad-Gita describe the various duties of man.

The history of Gaytri's family

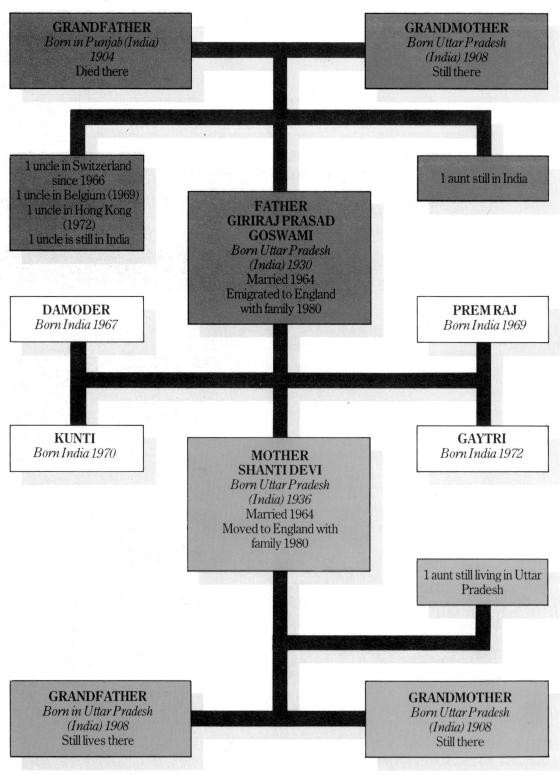

GRANDFATHER
Born in Punjab (India)
1904
Died there

GRANDMOTHER
Born Uttar Pradesh (India) 1908
Still there

1 uncle in Switzerland since 1966
1 uncle in Belgium (1969)
1 uncle in Hong Kong (1972)
1 uncle is still in India

FATHER
GIRIRAJ PRASAD GOSWAMI
Born Uttar Pradesh (India) 1930
Married 1964
Emigrated to England with family 1980

1 aunt still in India

DAMODER
Born India 1967

PREM RAJ
Born India 1969

KUNTI
Born India 1970

GAYTRI
Born India 1972

MOTHER
SHANTI DEVI
Born Uttar Pradesh (India) 1936
Married 1964
Moved to England with family 1980

1 aunt still living in Uttar Pradesh

GRANDFATHER
Born in Uttar Pradesh (India) 1908
Still lives there

GRANDMOTHER
Born Uttar Pradesh (India) 1908
Still there

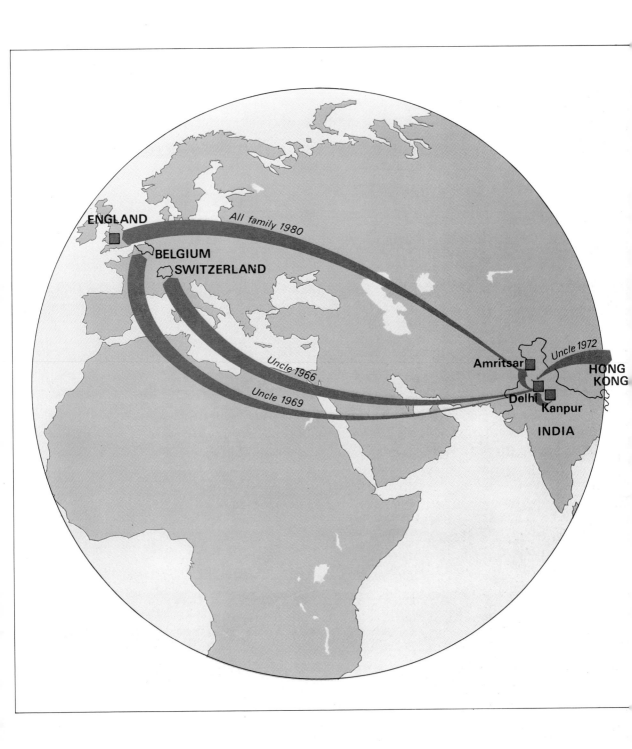

ENGLAND

BELGIUM
SWITZERLAND

All family 1980

Uncle 1966

Uncle 1969

Amritsar

Uncle 1972

HONG
KONG

Delhi

Kanpur

INDIA

What a Hindu wears

My mother and father wear the same type of clothes they wore in India. I only wear a sari on special occasions.

There are no special Hindu clothes. A person wears the clothes of the family birthplace or what is best for the country in which they live. In Britain most men wear western clothes. Most women still prefer to wear the traditional Indian dress – the sari.

My mother has taught me how to put on a sari in the proper way.

A sari is made from one piece of cloth that is between 43″ (110 cm) and 55″ (140 cm) wide and 16½ feet (5 m) to 20 feet (8 m) long. The cloth is wrapped around the waist and tucked into a petticoat to form a skirt. The rest of the cloth is put over the top of the body and shoulder in different styles according to the family birthplace in India. Many Indian women wear a jewel in their nose and many bracelets.

Eating the Hindu way

My family does not eat meat. We go to shops where they sell special Indian vegetables, herbs and spices.

Many Hindus from Northern India are vegetarians as it is thought wrong to kill animals. Hinduism teaches respect for all forms of life. Some Hindus do eat meat but not beef. The cow is a holy animal to Hindus. Vegetables are prepared in many different ways. Many herbs and spices are used to give flavor.

My mother still cooks the same kind of food we had in India. I like the curries, but not too hot!

Each part of India has its own special cooking. The meal shown here includes puri – a type of bread fried in butter, matar-panir – a vegetable curry with peas and curd cheese, rice and pédā – made out of milk, sugar and nuts. Hindus have many rules about how to eat. Cleanliness is very important and some will only eat with people of their own class.

A Hindu wedding

At my uncle's wedding my cousin Shankar acted as his attendant. We all wore traditional clothes.

It is the Hindu custom for the parents to arrange a marriage. The parents try to find someone of a similar type of family. A priest then looks at the horoscopes of the couple to fix a date and time for the wedding. The father of the bride has to give money called a dowry to the bridegroom.

There are many ceremonies at a wedding and the feast afterwards can last for three days.

Each family has its own priest who builds a sacred fire. The father gives the bride to the bridegroom. They promise to respect each other. Then they take seven steps in a circle around the sacred fire. They ask for success as well as friendship in their marriage. Then the priest chants mantras – holy hymns. After the feast the bride leaves her parents' home in a ceremony called Vida and becomes part of her husband's family.

Customs and festivals

We have many celebrations and festivals each year. I look forward to them very much.

Hindu festivals are happy occasions. The first event in a Hindu's life is the name-giving ceremony. This has to take place before the first birthday. The child is fed its first spoon of rice. A major festival each year is Divali, in honor of Rama. Homes are lit by lamps, candles and even sparklers. Firework displays are also held.

One of my favorite festivals is Holi when we throw colored powder and water at each other.

Many Hindu festivals celebrate the start of a season of the year. Holi is the start of spring. It also remembers the gods Radha and Krishna who were happy lovers. Navaratri, a nine-day festival in the autumn, is dedicated to Durga and celebrates motherhood. Raksha Bandhan is the festival of protection. Girls tie a symbol called a rakhi on a brother's wrist in return for his protection.

The Hindu year

Hindus use the lunar calendar which means that the months start with each new moon. The first month of the year is Vaisakha and New Year's day is in the first or second week of April.

NOVEMBER — KARTTIKA
DECEMBER — MARGASIRSHA
OCTOBER — ASVINA
SEPTEMBER — BHADRAPADA
AUGUST — SHRAVAN
JULY — ASHADHA

DEEPAVALI
(DIWALI)
Karttika – 5 days of which the 3rd day is the most important
Means 'the row of lights'. At this time Rama returned to his kingdom after a 14 year banishment. Commonly known as the Festival of Light.

VIJAYA DASHAMI
(DASHEHRA)
Asvina – 1 day
Celebrates the triumph of Good over Evil. On this day Rama defeated the ten-headed Ravana.

NAVARATRI
Asvina – 9 days
Festival devoted to Durga, the symbol of motherhood.

GANESHA CHATURTHI
Bhadrapada – 1 day
Festival of Ganesha, the God of Good Omen with the elephant head. Particularly celebrated in Maharashtra.

ONAM
Bhadrapada – 1 day
Harvest festival. The most important festival in Kerala.

RAKSHA BANDHAN
Shravan – 1 day
Festival of protection which celebrates Indra, the king of the heavens, being protected by a rakhi when fighting demons. On this day girls tie a rakhi on a brother's wrist in return for his protection.

JANMA ASHTAMI
Shravan – 1 day
The birthday of Krishna, Vishnu's reincarnation. Celebrated all over India, especially in Krishna's childhood homes.

RATH YATRA
Ashadha – 1 day
The festival is held in Puri in Orissa in honour of Lord Jagannath (Lord of the Universe).

MAGHA FEBRUARY

PHALGUNA MARCH

CHAITRA APRIL

VAISAKHA MAY

JYESTHA

JUNE

BIRTHDAY OF SWAMI VIVEKANANDA
Pausa – 1 day
Founder of Aryasmaj, a branch of Hinduism. His birthday is celebrated all over India.

SARASWATI PUJA
Magha – 1 day
Celebration in honour of Saraswati, the Goddess of Knowledge.

PONGAL
(SANKRANTI)
Magha – 3 days
Harvest festival. In Southern India the sun is worshipped on the first day, and elsewhere cattle are honoured.

HOLI
Phalguna – 1 day
Celebrates Spring. A happy festival when people often throw coloured powder and water over each other.

SHIVARATRI
Phalguna – 1 day
For all Hindus a solemn festival devoted to the worship of Shiva.

UGADI
(NEW YEAR)
Chaitra – 1 day
The Hindu New Year according to the lunar calendar.

PURAM
Vaisakha – 1 day
In Kerala in India there is an impressive festival at the temple of Shiva. It ends with firework displays.

RAM NAVAMI
Vaisakha – 1 day
The birthday of Rama, held on the 9th day of the month. It is a day of fasting and readings are made from the Ramayana.

VAISAKHI
Vaisakha – 1 day
This is the beginning of the solar New Year and is observed all over the UK. The River Ganges is believed to have been created on this day.

Hindu facts and figures

Hinduism is the third largest religion in the world with about 550 million followers. The largest is Christianity with about one billion and then Islam with about 600 million followers.

The great majority of Hindus live in India where over 80% of the population follow the religion. In Pakistan only 11% are Hindus. Hindus are found in many other parts of the world. East Africa has the largest number in one area outside India and Pakistan. There are also communities in Sri Lanka, Nepal, Bali in Indonesia, Europe, Canada and the USA.

In the United States there are about 300,000 Hindus. Most of them came from India and Pakistan.

Hinduism is the world's oldest major religion. It can be traced back to at least 2500 BC in the Indus Valley in India. The oldest Holy Book, the Rig Veda, was compiled by about 1000 BC. The Holy Books include the four Vedas – Rig, Sama, Yajur and Atharvan, the Upanishads, the Ramayana and the Mahabharata which includes a famous section called the Bhagavad-Gita.

The main Hindu beliefs include:

The unity of all things in the world. The spirit of God, Brahman, is said to run through everything in the world – plants, animals and humans.

Ahimsa – the belief that it is wrong to hurt any living thing.

Samsara – the cycle of life and death. One is reborn into another form after death until the highest state, called Moksha, is achieved through a perfect life.

Karma – a person's behavior and actions in this life will decide their next life.

Dharma – a person has certain duties to family, class and to God.

Hinduism divides humans into social groups or castes. People are born into their caste. The four main classes of caste, in order of importance, are Brahmins – priests, Kshatriyas – warriors and rulers, Vaishyas – merchants and farmers and Shudras – peasants and laborers. A further class called Untouchables did all the very unpleasant work. Today the strict divisions of the caste system are being ignored by many Hindus.

Glossary

Bhagavad-Gita A Holy Book also known as "The Song of God." It is a long poem in which God takes the form of Krishna.

Brahman The Hindu word for God. The origin and essence of the universe.

Brahmin The priest class of Hindu society.

Dowry Money or goods given by the bride's father to the bridegroom on marriage.

Ganges The holy river of India.

Ganesha The elephant-headed god who is prayed to for success in new ventures and business.

Gayatri A holy hymn to the sun found in one of the Vedas.

Hindu A person who follows the Hindu religion. It was first used by ancient Persians to describe the people living by the River Indus in the Punjab in India.

Krishna A god who appeared on earth to save mankind – known also as the god of love.

Mandir A Hindu temple.

Moksha Freedom from the cycle of life and death and unity with God.

Prasada Holy food shared with the gods during worship.

Sanskrit The ancient language in which the Hindu Holy Books are written.

Sari The traditional dress of Indian women made from one piece of cloth.

Shiva The god who rules life and death. The destroyer and creator of all things in the world.

Vedas Four Holy Books which are the oldest written statements on Hindu belief. The Rig Veda was compiled about 1000 BC.

Vegetarian A person who does not eat meat.

Upanishads Holy Books which contain many of the most important statements of the Hindu religion. Compiled about 500 BC.

Vishnu A kind and gentle god who aids mankind to escape the forces of evil.

31

Index